MoshiMoshiKawaii ®

The Strawberry Moshi Collection

Where is Strawberry Moshi?

Where is Strawberry Princess Moshi?

Where is Strawberry Mermaid Moshi?

WALKER BOOKS
AND SUBSIDIARIES
LONDON · BOSTON · SYDNEY · AUCKLAND

Where is Strawberry Moshi?

How to Play

Strawberry Moshi

Super Moshi

Moshi Town is a wonderland teeming with all sorts of cute Moshi dressed up in colourful outfits. Strawberry Moshi is looking for her sweetheart, Super Moshi, but Moshi Town is so busy that she will need your help to find him.

Strawberry Moshi and **Super Moshi** are in every scene. Find them in busy Moshi Town. Look carefully, because there are Moshi who look almost the same as **Strawberry Moshi** and **Super Moshi.**

See what other funny Moshi you can find in each picture. Take a close look at their faces and the clothes they're wearing. Look out for the giant Maze Moshi in the middle of the story!

At the end of the book, there are more Moshi for you to go back and look for. Find out what adventures they have been on.

Meet the Moshi

and all their friends!

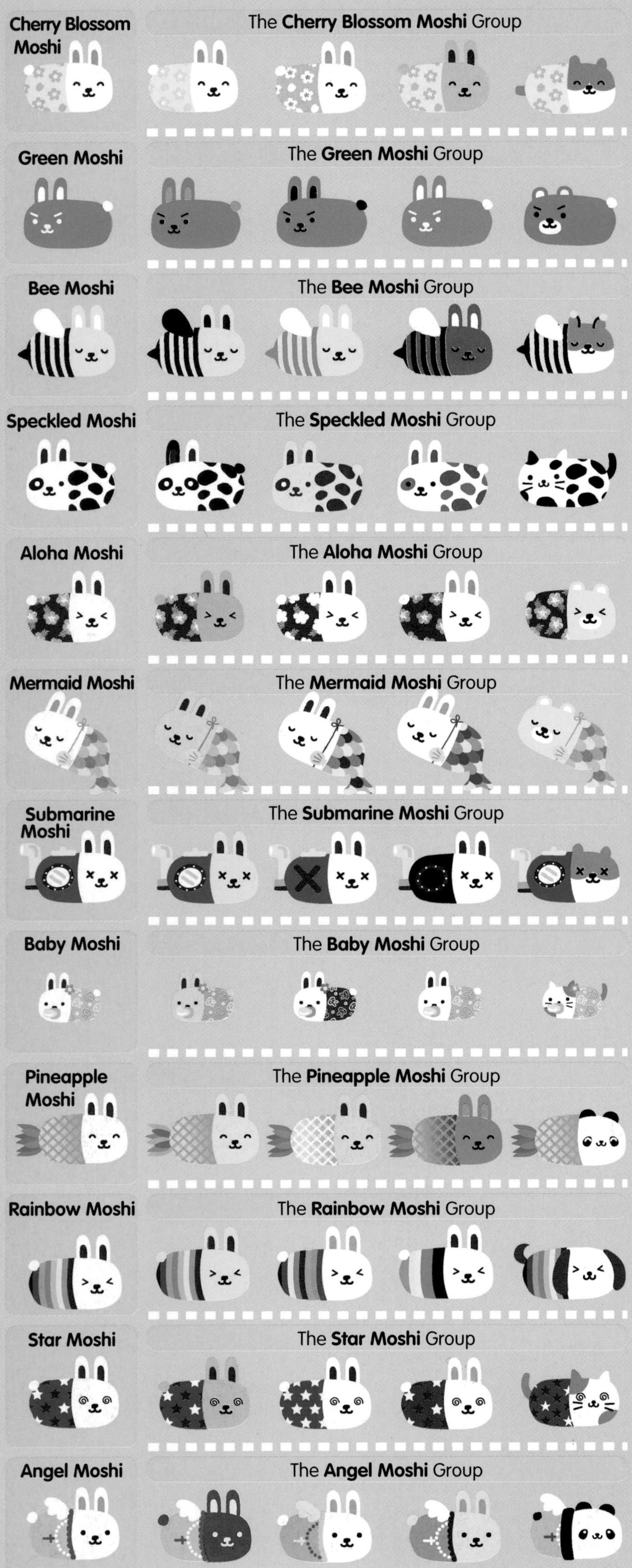
Cherry Blossom Moshi
The Cherry Blossom Moshi Group
Green Moshi
The Green Moshi Group
Bee Moshi
The Bee Moshi Group
Speckled Moshi
The Speckled Moshi Group
Aloha Moshi
The Aloha Moshi Group
Mermaid Moshi
The Mermaid Moshi Group
Submarine Moshi
The Submarine Moshi Group
Baby Moshi
The Baby Moshi Group
Pineapple Moshi
The Pineapple Moshi Group
Rainbow Moshi
The Rainbow Moshi Group
Star Moshi
The Star Moshi Group
Angel Moshi
The Angel Moshi Group

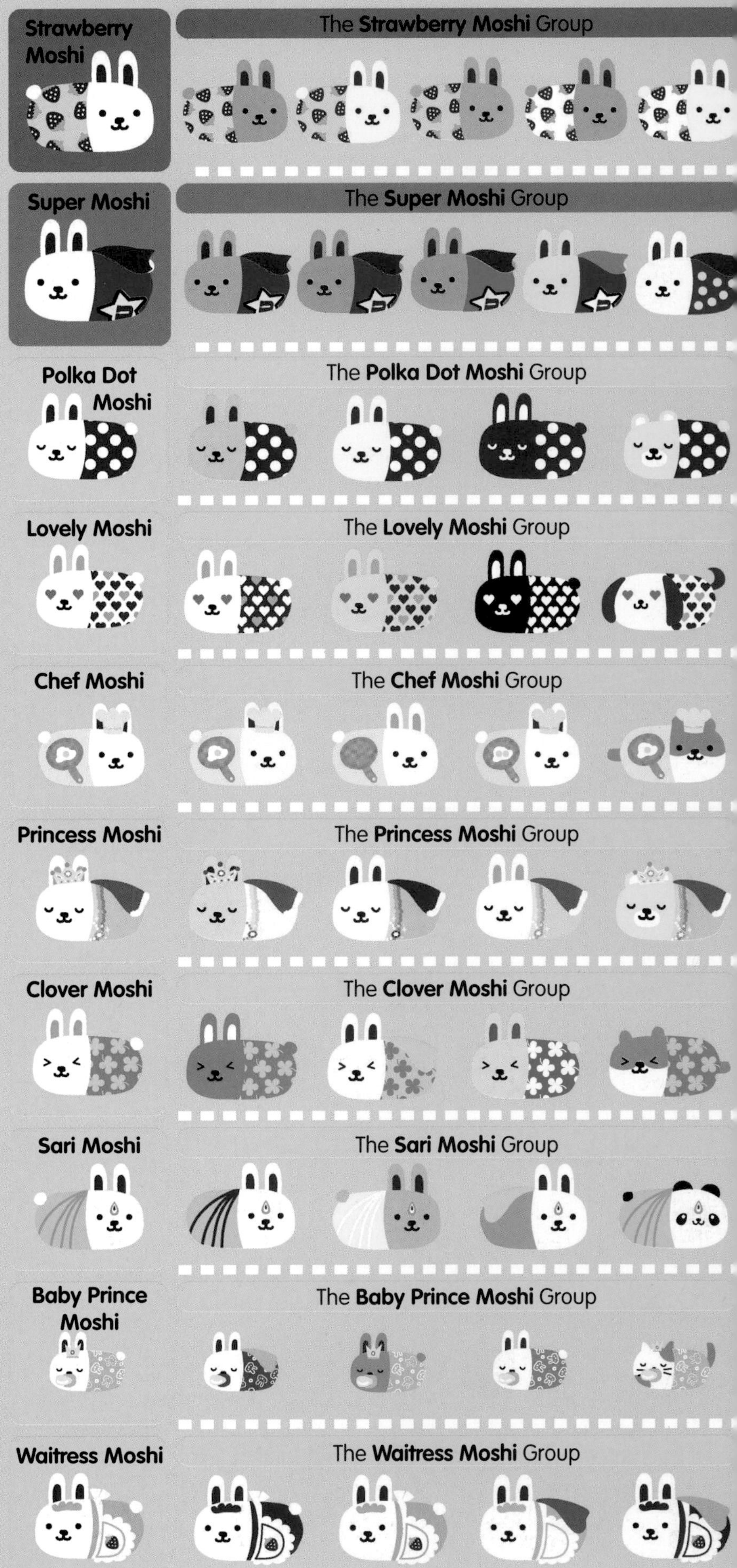
Strawberry Moshi
The Strawberry Moshi Group
Super Moshi
The Super Moshi Group
Polka Dot Moshi
The Polka Dot Moshi Group
Lovely Moshi
The Lovely Moshi Group
Chef Moshi
The Chef Moshi Group
Princess Moshi
The Princess Moshi Group
Clover Moshi
The Clover Moshi Group
Sari Moshi
The Sari Moshi Group
Baby Prince Moshi
The Baby Prince Moshi Group
Waitress Moshi
The Waitress Moshi Group

At first glance, all the Moshi look the same. Look again and you'll see they are all different! Find each type in the book.

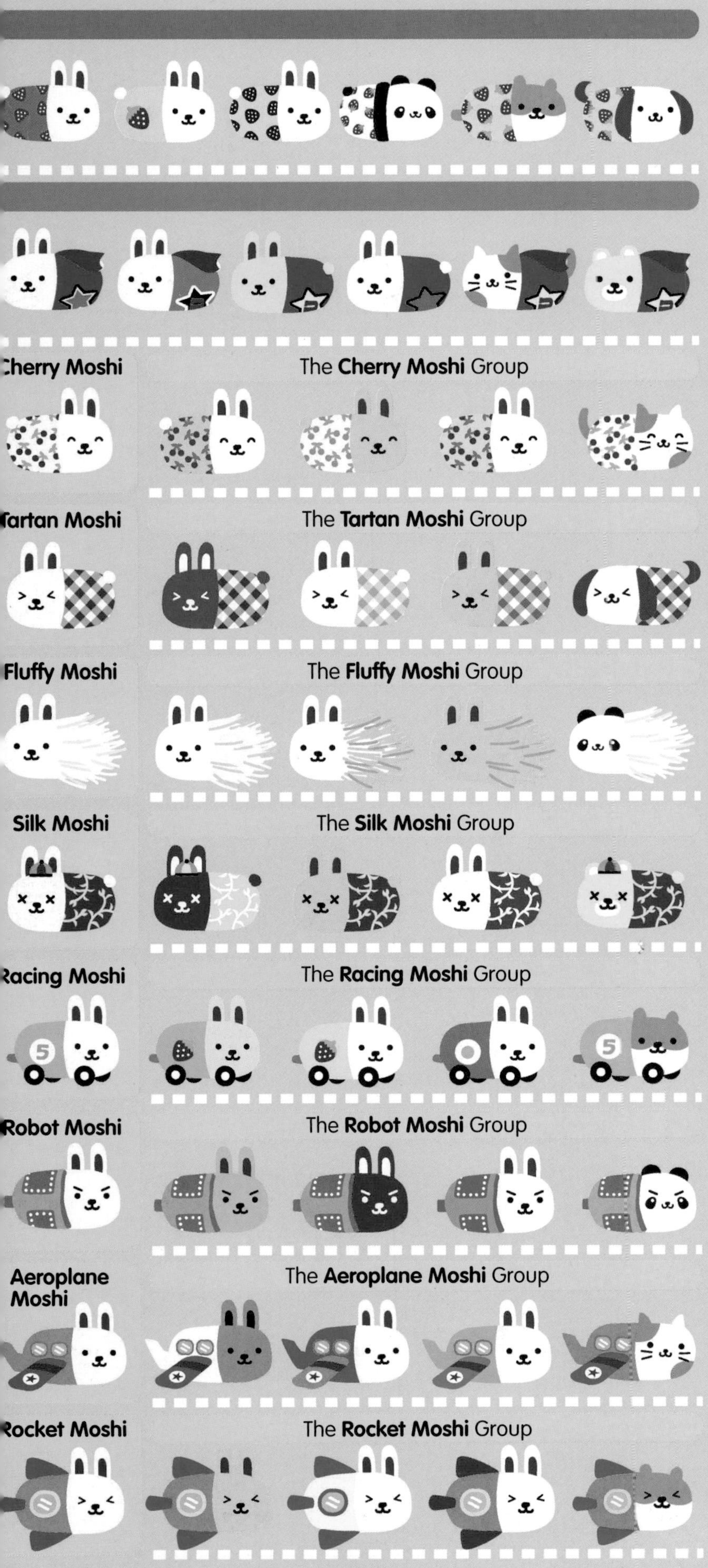
Cherry Moshi
The Cherry Moshi Group
Tartan Moshi
The Tartan Moshi Group
Fluffy Moshi
The Fluffy Moshi Group
Silk Moshi
The Silk Moshi Group
Racing Moshi
The Racing Moshi Group
Robot Moshi
The Robot Moshi Group
Aeroplane Moshi
The Aeroplane Moshi Group
Rocket Moshi
The Rocket Moshi Group

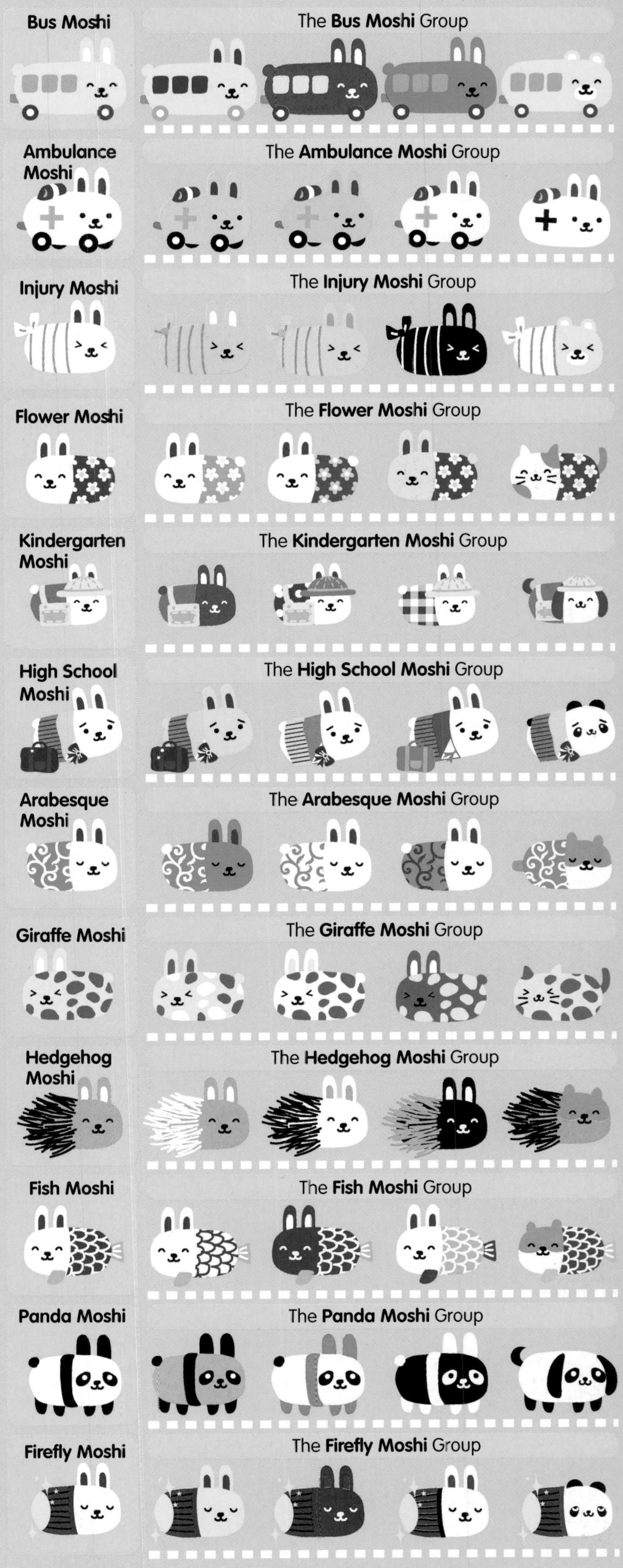
Bus Moshi
The Bus Moshi Group
Ambulance Moshi
The Ambulance Moshi Group
Injury Moshi
The Injury Moshi Group
Flower Moshi
The Flower Moshi Group
Kindergarten Moshi
The Kindergarten Moshi Group
High School Moshi
The High School Moshi Group
Arabesque Moshi
The Arabesque Moshi Group
Giraffe Moshi
The Giraffe Moshi Group
Hedgehog Moshi
The Hedgehog Moshi Group
Fish Moshi
The Fish Moshi Group
Panda Moshi
The Panda Moshi Group
Firefly Moshi
The Firefly Moshi Group

Strawberry Moshi is in Mushroom Forest. She is looking for her sweetheart, **Super Moshi.**

Where is **Strawberry Moshi?**

Where is **Super Moshi?**

Find these other Moshi. What are they doing?

Cherry Blossom Moshi, you have gathered a lot of flowers.

Why are you angry, **Green Moshi**?

You are buzzing happily, **Bee Moshi**.

Who is watching you, **Speckled Moshi**?

Aloha Moshi, where are you off to with your snorkel?

Strawberry Moshi did not find **Super Moshi** in Mushroom Forest, so she has come to **Mermaid Moshi Sea** to look for him.

Where is **Strawberry Moshi**?

Where is **Super Moshi**?

Find these other Moshi. What are they doing?

Mermaid Moshi, you like listening to the sound of the waves.

What are you looking at, **Submarine Moshi?**

Baby Moshi, you can swim like a fish!

Pineapple Moshi, you love the surprises under the sea.

Rainbow Moshi, where are you off to on your surfboard?

START

FINISH

Delicious Land

ICE CREAM

Scary Land

Suddenly, a giant **Maze Moshi** pops out of the sea. Find a path through the maze to wonderful **Delicious Land.** But be careful you don't end up in **Scary Land**!

Trace a path through Maze Moshi with your finger. Can you reach Delicious Land?

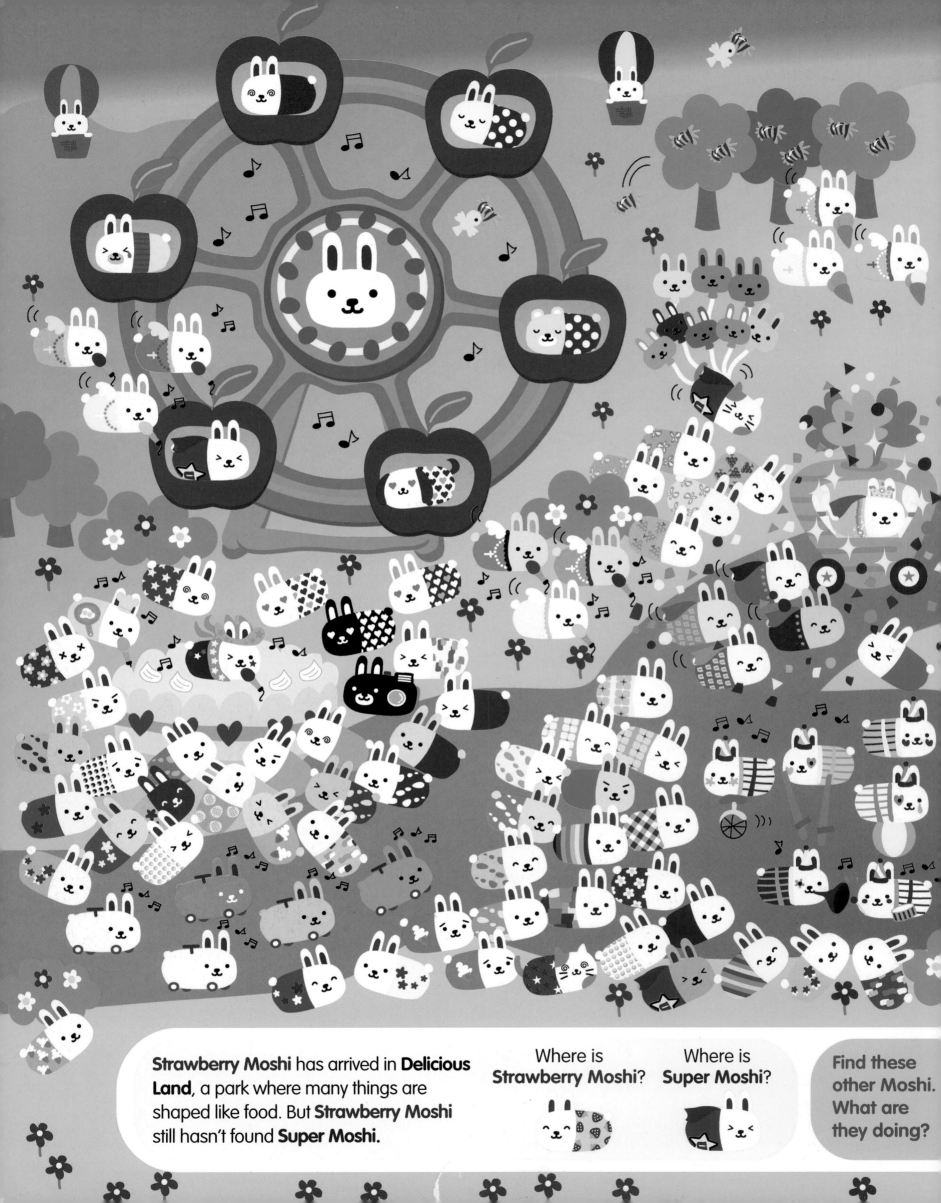

Strawberry Moshi has arrived in **Delicious Land,** a park where many things are shaped like food. But **Strawberry Moshi** still hasn't found **Super Moshi.**

Where is **Strawberry Moshi**?

Where is **Super Moshi**?

Find these other Moshi. What are they doing?

RACING STADIUM

Strawberry Café

ICE CREAM

Star Moshi, you look dizzy!

Is the ice cream good, **Angel Moshi**?

Polka Dot Moshi, is that your boyfriend?

Lovely Moshi, who are you in love with?

Chef Moshi, where are you taking that carrot?

Strawberry Moshi is in **Castle Carrot**, where lots of the Moshi are wearing capes. Will **Strawberry Moshi** be able to find **Super Moshi** in his cape?

Where is **Strawberry Moshi**?

Where is **Super Moshi**?

Find these other Moshi. What are they doing?

Strawberry Café

Princess Moshi, you have a beautiful necklace.

Clover Moshi, you look surprised to see your friend.

Sari Moshi, you have a fantastic flying carpet.

Baby Prince Moshi, it's time for your milk!

Don't spill the juice, **Waitress Moshi!**

Menu

Strawberry Parfait

Carrot Parfait

Strawberry Juice

Carrot Juice

Hot Strawberry Milk

Strawberry Moshi has not found her beloved **Super Moshi** yet. She is having a snack at **Strawberry Café** with her friends.

Where is **Strawberry Moshi**?

Where is **Super Moshi**?

Find these other Moshi. What are they doing?

Isn't the baby cute, **Cherry Moshi**?

Tartan Moshi, watch your step!

Fluffy Moshi, the carrot parfait must taste good.

Thanks for your help, **Silk Moshi!**

Racing Moshi, where are you off to in such in a hurry?

Super Moshi is at the Racing Stadium, and **Strawberry Moshi** has come to look for him. Watch out, racers! *CRASH!*

Where is **Strawberry Moshi**?

Where is **Super Moshi**?

Find these other Moshi. What are they doing?

Go on, **Robot Moshi!**

Aeroplane Moshi, spread your wings and fly!

You're nearly there, **Rocket Moshi!**

Bus Moshi, you've still got a chance!

Ambulance Moshi, please hurry up!

BATTERY CHARGER

START

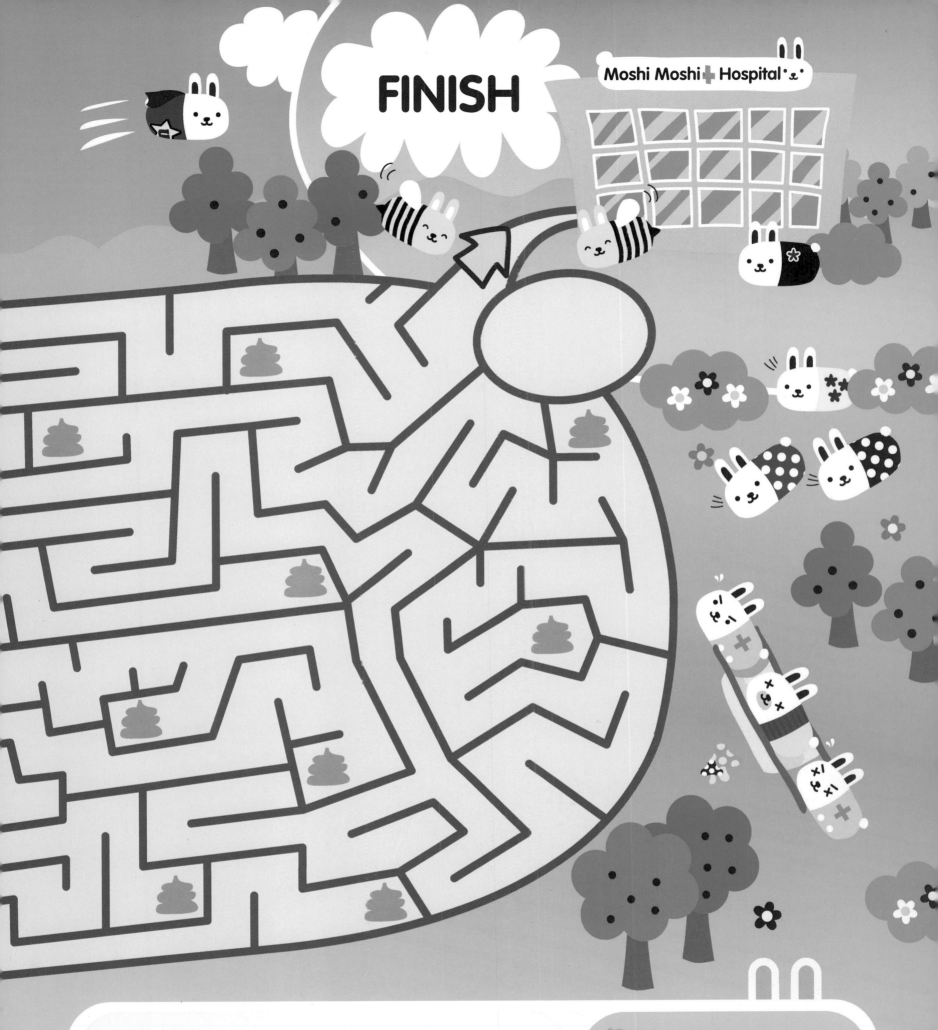

FINISH

Moshi Moshi + Hospital

Ambulance Moshi is rushing the injured Moshi to the hospital. But here is **Maze Moshi** again! They need to quickly find a path through the maze to the hospital.

Find your way through the maze. Watch out for messes on the way!

Moshi Moshi

Still searching for **Super Moshi**, **Strawberry Moshi** follows the trail to **Moshi Moshi Hospital**.

Where is **Strawberry Moshi**?

Where is **Super Moshi**?

Find these other Moshi. What are they doing?

Hospital

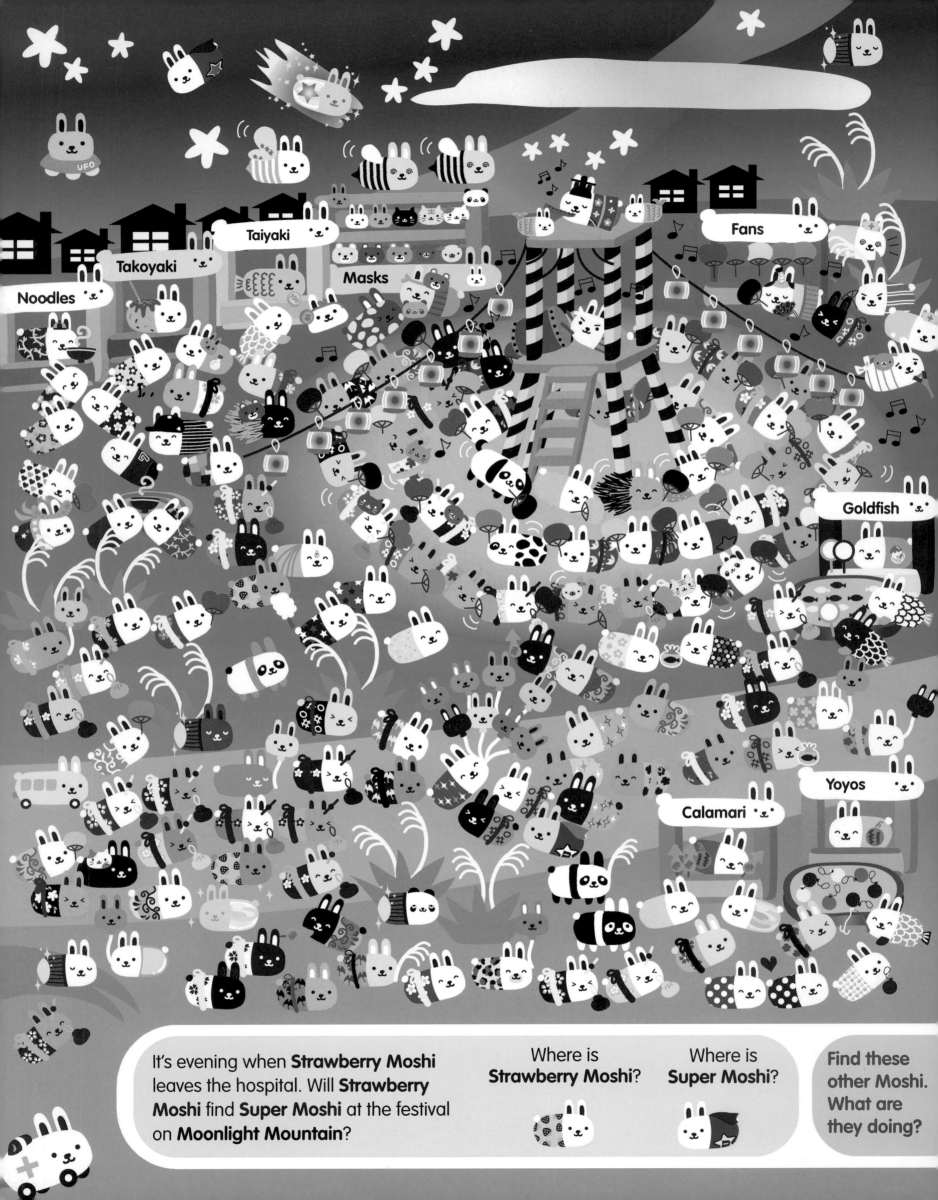

Noodles

Takoyaki

Taiyaki

Masks

Fans

Goldfish

Calamari

Yoyos

It's evening when **Strawberry Moshi** leaves the hospital. Will **Strawberry Moshi** find **Super Moshi** at the festival on **Moonlight Mountain**?

Where is **Strawberry Moshi**?

Where is **Super Moshi**?

Find these other Moshi. What are they doing?

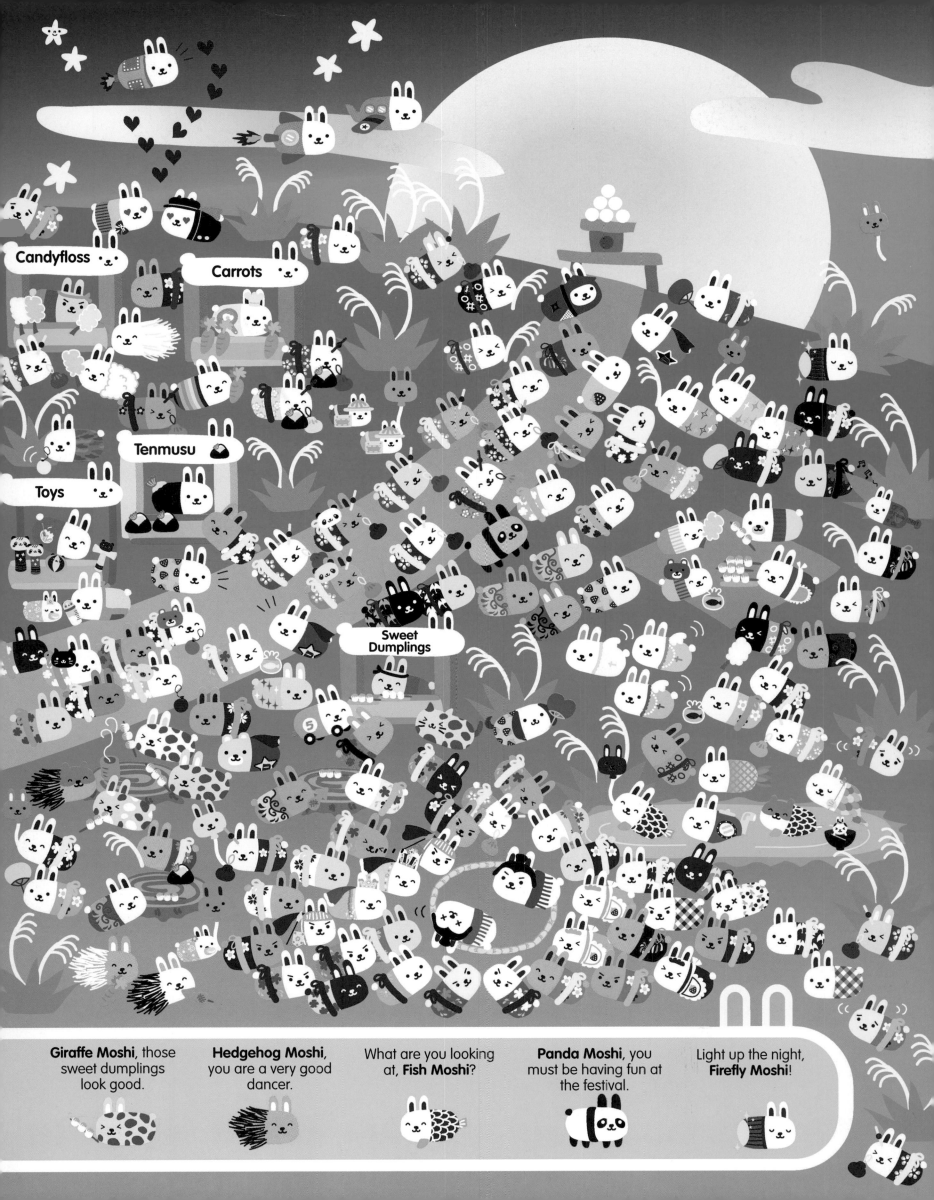

Candyfloss

Carrots

Tenmusu

Toys

Sweet Dumplings

Giraffe Moshi, those sweet dumplings look good.

Hedgehog Moshi, you are a very good dancer.

What are you looking at, **Fish Moshi**?

Panda Moshi, you must be having fun at the festival.

Light up the night, **Firefly Moshi**!

Keep on searching!

Here are even more Moshi to find. Look again at each scene to see if you can spot them.

 This is **Oyaji Moshi.** He is in every scene. Follow his story through from the beginning.

 Mushroom Forest

 Mermaid Moshi Sea

 Maze Moshi

 Delicious Land

 Castle Carrot

 Strawberry Café

 Racing Stadium

 Maze Moshi

 Moshi Moshi Hospital

 Moonlight Mountain

And look again for these Moshi and their trinkets.

Mushroom Forest

Kappa Moshi

Three Little Pig Moshi

Little Samurai Moshi

Red Riding Hood Moshi

 Wicked Witch Moshi

Mermaid Moshi Sea

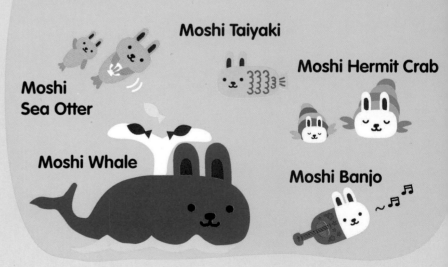

Moshi Taiyaki

Moshi Hermit Crab

Moshi Sea Otter

Moshi Whale

Moshi Banjo

Delicious Land

Moshi Letter Box

Moshi Purse

Camera Moshi

Moshi Balloon

Moshi Bench

Castle Carrot

King Moshi

Tuxedo Moshi

Knight Moshi

Present Moshi

Cleaner Moshi

Strawberry Café

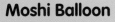

Cake Moshi
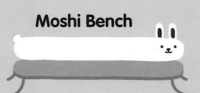

Moshi Cookies

Moshi Shaved Ice

Moshi Pudding

Moshi Baby Bottle

Racing Stadium

Moshi UFO

Moshi Mobile

Firecracker Moshi

Moshi Onigiri

Moshi Battery Charger

BATTERY CHARGER

Moshi Moshi Hospital

Moshi Syringe

Moshi Plaster

Moshi Radio

Moshi Pillow
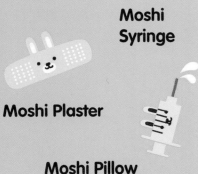

Moshi Plant

Moonlight Mountain

Flute Player Moshi

Sumo Moshi

Shooting Star Moshi

Tenmusu Moshi

Takayaki Moshi

Where is Strawberry Princess Moshi?

Frill Moshi

My dress has three frills.

The Frill Moshi Group

Meet the Moshi
and all their friends!

Polka Dot Moshi

My outfit has white polka dots.

The Polka Dot Moshi Group

Strawberry Moshi

I wear a strawberry outfit and become Strawberry Princess Moshi when I dress up.

The Strawberry Moshi Group

Lovely Moshi

I am covered in little hearts.

The Lovely Moshi Group

Strawberry Princess Moshi

I wear a strawberry-patterned dress and a ribbon.

The Strawberry Princess Moshi Group

Aloha Panda

My costume has blue flowers on it.

The Aloha Panda Group

Cinderella Moshi

I wear a sparkly blue dress.

The Cinderella Moshi Group

Shop Assistant Moshi

I wear a ribbon around my neck.

The Shop Assistant Moshi Group

Snow White Moshi

I wear a ribbon and carry a red apple.

The Snow White Moshi Group

Mermaid Moshi

I wear a shell bikini.

The Mermaid Moshi Group

At first glance, each Moshi looks the same. Look again and you'll see they're all different. Find each type in the book.

Butterfly Moshi

I have starry wings.

The Butterfly Moshi Group

Deer Moshi

My antlers are cute.

The Deer Moshi Group

Toadstool Neko

My costume is decorated with toadstools.

The Toadstool Neko Group

Knight Moshi

I wear a cool suit of armour and a cape.

The Knight Moshi Group

Waitress Moshi

I wear an apron with a strawberry on.

The Waitress Moshi Group

Present Moshi

I am tied up with a lovely ribbon.

The Present Moshi Group

Cinderella's Town

Crown Prince Moshi is throwing a grand ball tonight. **Strawberry Moshi** has come to find her friends and a dress to wear.

Where is **Strawberry Moshi**?

Where is **Cinderella Moshi**?

Where is **Snow White Moshi**?

Strawberry Boutique

Strawberry Moshi has come to **Strawberry Boutique** to find the perfect strawberry dress.

Where is **Strawberry Moshi**?

Where is **Cinderella Moshi**?

Where is **Snow White Moshi**?

Where are these Moshi?

Frill Moshi, you are chatting.

Are you with your sweetheart, **Polka Dot Moshi?**

Lovely Moshi, you are keeping a straight face.

Aloha Panda, have you found your favourite?

Shop Assistant Moshi, you look very busy.

1

Someone has lost their purse. Can you find it?

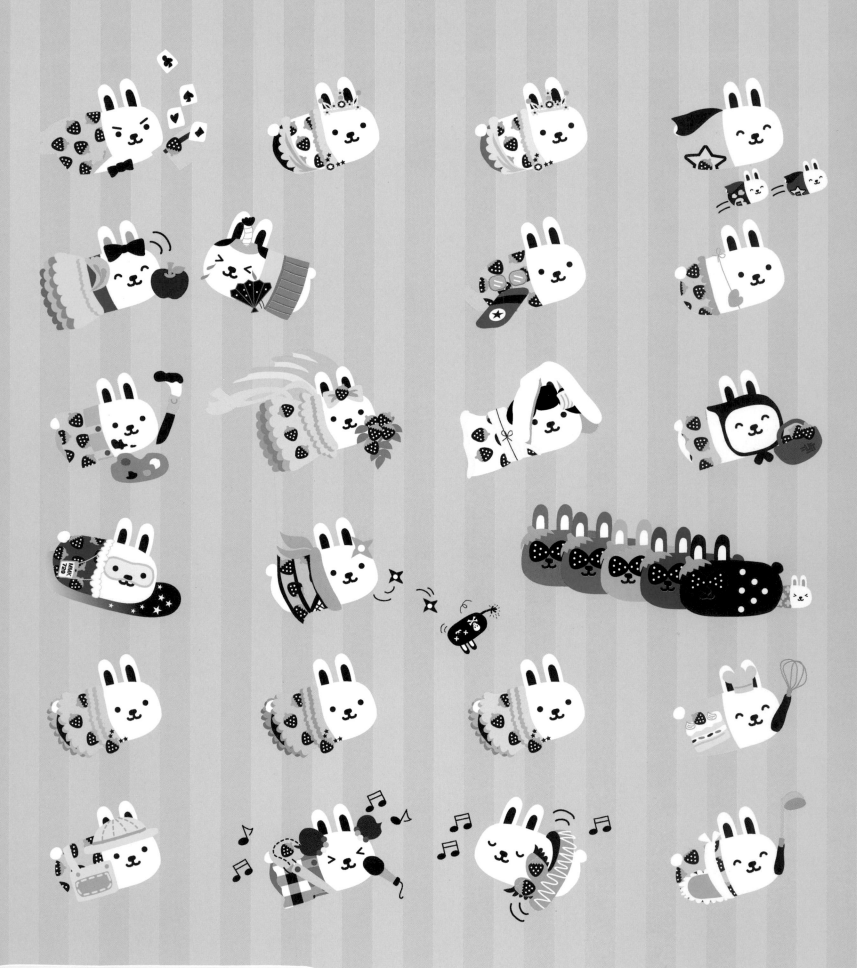

The Changing Room

Strawberry Moshi has finally chosen the dress to turn her into **Strawberry Princess Moshi**.

Where is **Strawberry Princess Moshi**?

Where is **Cinderella Moshi**?

Where is **Snow White Moshi**?

Where are these Moshi?

To The Castle

It's time for the ball! Everyone is heading to **Crown Prince Moshi**'s castle.

Where is **Strawberry Princess Moshi**?

Where is **Cinderella Moshi**?

Where is **Snow White Moshi**?

Where are these Moshi?

Are you having a rest, **Mermaid Moshi**?

Butterfly Moshi, look out!

Enjoy your picnic, **Deer Moshi**.

Toadstool Neko, those mushrooms look good.

Knight Moshi, you are welcoming the guests!

2

There are two balls in the picture. Can you find them?

Hurry up, **Waitress Moshi**.

Present Moshi, you are enchanting.

Jewel Moshi, you dance so well.

Cherry Inu, you are enjoying the food.

Devil Moshi, you are casting a magic spell!

3

There are three mirrors in the picture. Can you find them?

START

Devil Moshi Cave

It's so cold inside the **Devil Moshi Cave** that the Moshi have turned into ice cubes. Is **Strawberry Princess Moshi** all right?

Where is **Strawberry Princess Moshi**?

Where is **Cinderella Moshi**?

Where is **Snow White Moshi**?

Where are these Moshi?

Tartan Moshi, who have you knocked into?

What are you writing, **Injury Moshi?**

Speckled Moshi, look out for the Devil Moshi.

Wave your flag, **Star Kuma.**

Enjoy the slide, **Hedgehog Moshi.**

There are five bats flying in the picture. Can you find them?

5

Which is **Firefly Moshi's** shadow?

Which is **Racing Moshi's** shadow?

Which is **Submarine Moshi's** shadow?

Which is **Fish Moshi's** shadow?

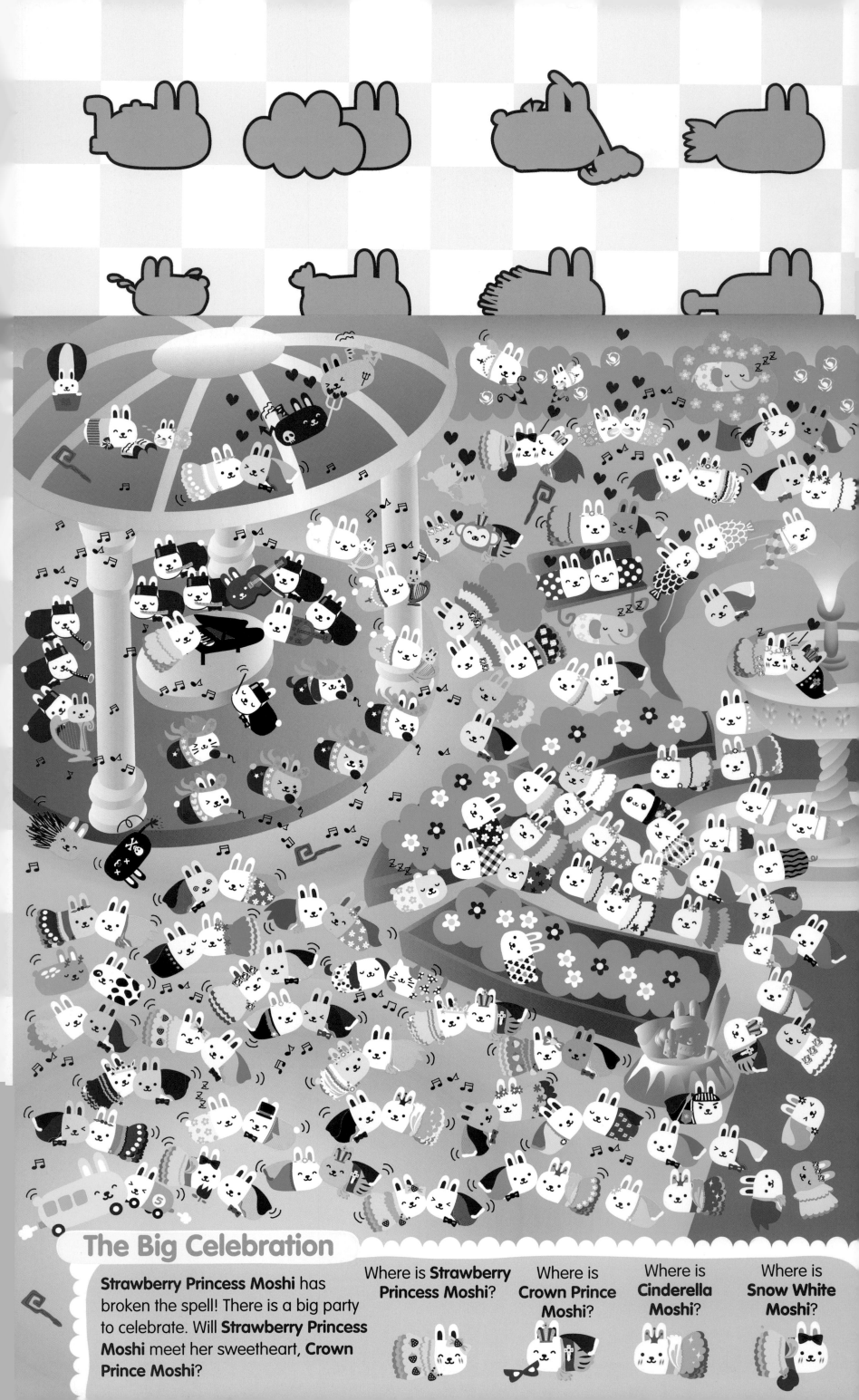

The Big Celebration

Strawberry Princess Moshi has broken the spell! There is a big party to celebrate. Will **Strawberry Princess Moshi** meet her sweetheart, **Crown Prince Moshi**?

Where is **Strawberry Princess Moshi**?

Where is **Crown Prince Moshi**?

Where is **Cinderella Moshi**?

Where is **Snow White Moshi**?

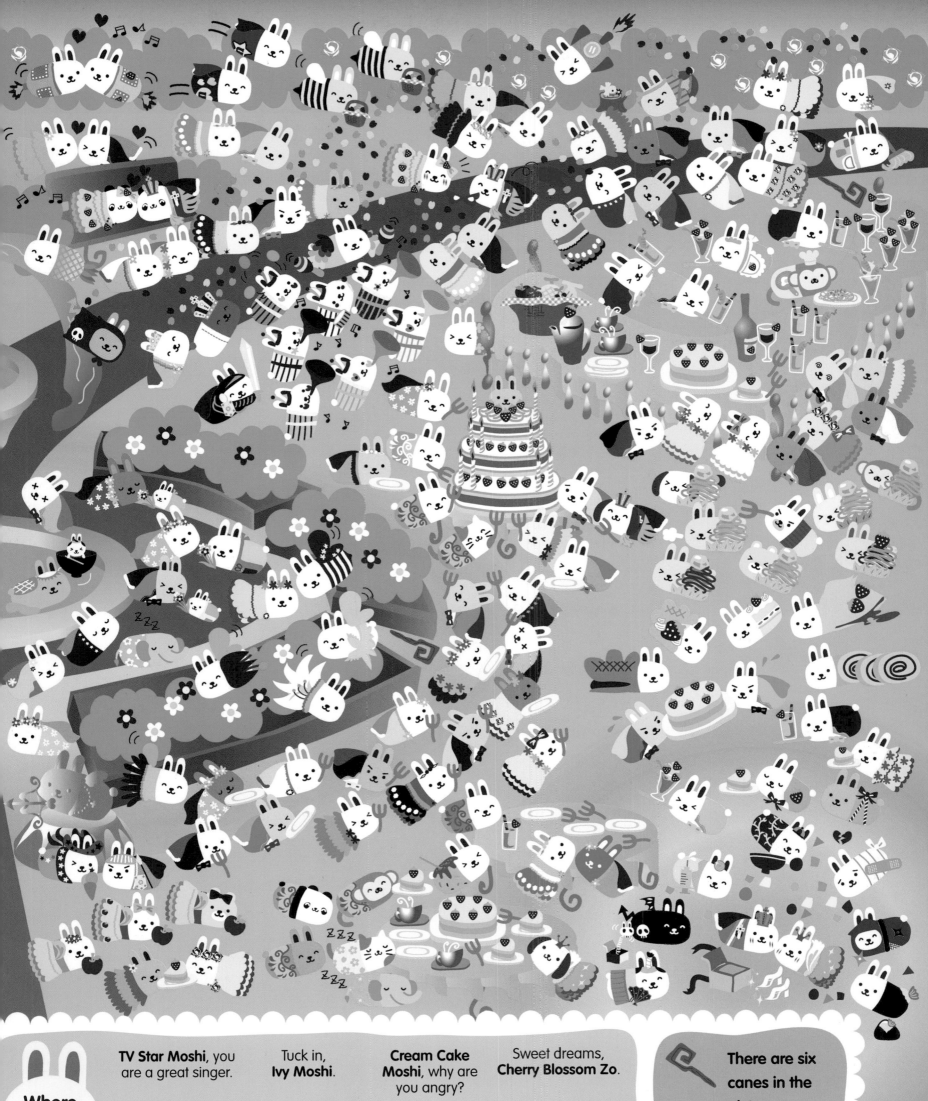

Where are these Moshi?

TV Star Moshi, you are a great singer.

Tuck in, **Ivy Moshi**.

Cream Cake Moshi, why are you angry?

Sweet dreams, **Cherry Blossom Zo**.

6 There are six canes in the picture. Can you find them?

The Flower Wedding

Moshi Love Stories

Follow the love stories of Strawberry Princess Moshi and her friends, from Cinderella's Town to The Flower Wedding.

Strawberry Princess Moshi

Cinderella's Town

A masked Moshi is looking at Strawberry Moshi.

Strawberry Boutique
And he is watching her in the boutique.

The Changing Room
Who is this mysterious Moshi?

To The Castle

He is still watching her…

The Prince's Ball

even when he dances with other Moshi.

The Bad Spell

The masked Moshi helps her when she's in danger.

The Secret Maze

And he is always right behind her.

Devil Moshi Cave

Who could this Moshi be?

The Shadow Game

Where has this mask come from?

The Big Celebration

The masked Moshi was Crown Prince Moshi!

The Flower Wedding

Crown Prince Moshi asks Strawberry Princess Moshi to marry him. It's the best day of Strawberry Princess Moshi's life!

Three cheers!

Cinderella Moshi

Cinderella's Town

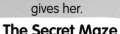

Cinderella Moshi has many admirers who offer her presents. But she turns down Injury Moshi when he offers her a plaster.

Strawberry Boutique

She also refuses the fan that Tono-sama Moshi gives her.

The Changing Room

She turns down the star that Ninja Moshi wants to give her.

To The Castle

She doesn't want Silk Moshi's noodles.

The Prince's Ball

She turns down Tenmusu Moshi's gift.

The Bad Spell

She says no when Oyaji Moshi tries to give her a doll.

The Secret Maze

She does not want a jack-in-the-box either.

Devil Moshi Cave

She certainly does not want Doctor Moshi's syringe.

The Shadow Game

Somebody is offering her a box…

The Big Celebration

inside is a pair of beautiful glass slippers!

The Flower Wedding

Cinderella Moshi loves the glass slippers and lives happily ever after with her Prince Moshi.

Snow White Moshi

Cinderella's Town

Kind **Snow White Moshi** gives an apple to anyone who needs cheering up, like Baby Moshi.

Strawberry Boutique

She makes Injury Moshi feel better.

The Changing Room

She comforts Tono-sama Moshi.

To The Castle

She wishes Ninja Moshi good luck.

The Prince's Ball

She tells Silk Moshi not to cry.

The Bad Spell

She wipes away Tenmusu Moshi's tears.

The Secret Maze

She accepts the apple Evil Witch Moshi gives her.

Devil Moshi Cave

She takes a bite and falls into a deep sleep.

The Shadow Game

Snow White Moshi will not wake up.

The Big Celebration

A prince wakes her with a kiss.

The Flower Wedding

The two marry and live happily ever after.

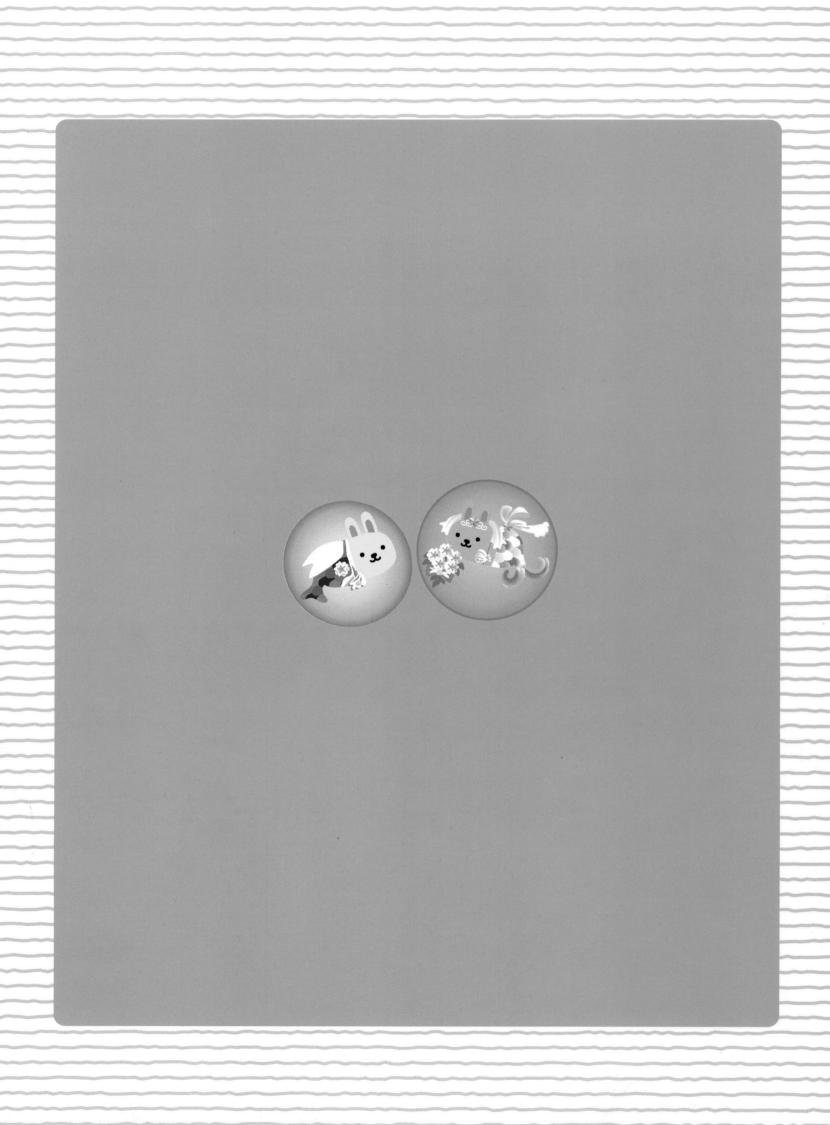

Where is Strawberry Mermaid Moshi ?

Meet the Moshi and all their friends!

Tropical Fish Moshi

My body has orange and white stripes.

The Tropical Fish Moshi Group

Tulip Moshi

My body is tulip-shaped.

The Tulip Moshi Group

Cinderella Moshi

I wear a sparkly blue dress.

The Cinderella Moshi Group

Lovely Kuma

I am covered in little hearts.

The Lovely Kuma Group

Diamond Ring Moshi

My precious jewel sparkles.

The Diamond Ring Moshi Group

Chef Moshi

I wear a tall chef's hat.

The Chef Moshi Group

Waitress Moshi

I wear an apron with a strawberry on.

The Waitress Moshi Group

Strawberry Moshi

I wear a strawberry outfit. I will dress up and transform into Strawberry Mermaid Moshi.

Strawberry Mermaid Moshi

I wear a strawberry bikini and a fancy starfish.

Mermaid Bride Moshi

I am a bride. I wear a white veil and carry a bouquet.

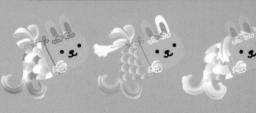

Mermaid Groom Moshi

Mermaid Bride Moshi's father

Angel Moshi

I can fly in the sky.

The Angel Moshi Group

At first glance all the Moshi look the same. Look again and you'll see they're all different! Find each type in the book.

The **Strawberry Mermaid Moshi** Group

The **Mermaid Bride Moshi** Group

Mermaid Bride Moshi's Family

Mermaid Bride Moshi's sisters

Cream Cake Neko

My body is a cream cake.

The **Cream Cake Neko** Group

Cake Moshi

My body is a strawberry cake.

The **Cake Moshi** Group

Ladybird Moshi

I wear a red and black dotty outfit.

The **Ladybird Moshi** Group

Bikini Moshi

I wear a heart-shaped bikini.

The **Bikini Moshi** Group

Carnation Moshi

I wear a flower petal skirt.

The **Carnation Moshi** Group

Baby Panda Moshi

I suck my dummy and wear a flower on my ear.

The **Baby Panda Moshi** Group

Pearl Moshi

My shiny pearls are very beautiful.

The **Pearl Moshi** Group

Pierrot Moshi

I wear a pointy hat and play the drum.

The **Pierrot Moshi** Group

The Underwater Chapel

It is **Mermaid Bride Moshi's** wedding day. **Strawberry Moshi** is dressed up as **Strawberry Mermaid Moshi**. Can you find the two friends?

Where is **Strawberry Mermaid Moshi**?

Where is **Mermaid Bride Moshi**?

The Flower Petal Walk

The wedding ceremony is about to begin in the wonderful flower-filled chapel. Where are the two friends?

Where is **Strawberry Mermaid Moshi**?

Where is **Mermaid Bride Moshi**?

Where are these Moshi?

What can you see through the window, **Tropical Fish Moshi**?

What lovely flowers, **Tulip Moshi**.

Cinderella Moshi, you are very chatty!

Lovely Kuma, were you taken by surprise?

Diamond Ring Moshi, you are praying.

Where are these trinkets?

Moshi Bag

Moshi Bouquet

The Busy Kitchen

Everyone in the kitchen is busy preparing the celebration banquet. Where are the two friends?

Where is **Strawberry Mermaid Moshi**?

Where is **Mermaid Bride Moshi**?

Where are these Moshi?

Chef Moshi, that looks delicious.

Waitress Moshi, you are very busy.

How do they taste, **Angel Moshi?**

Cream Cake Neko, have you lost your friends?

Cake Moshi, you are cutting neat slices.

Where are these trinkets?

Moshi Cookies

Moshi Frying Pan

The Wedding Banquet

Now the guests are all taking their places for the celebration banquet. Can you find the two friends?

Where is **Strawberry Mermaid Moshi**?

Where is **Mermaid Bride Moshi**?

Where are these Moshi?

Shake it, **Ladybird Moshi!**

Bikini Moshi, have you got your eye on someone?

Carnation Moshi, you are enjoying a glass of juice.

Baby Panda Moshi, you are too young to eat this food.

Pearl Moshi, be careful carrying that candle.

Where are these trinkets?

Moshi Harp

Moshi Blancmange

The Candlelit Garden

The party continues in the garden by candlelight. Where are the two friends?

Where is **Strawberry Mermaid Moshi**?

Where is **Mermaid Bride Moshi**?

Where are these Moshi?

Pierrot Moshi, you are playing music with your friends.

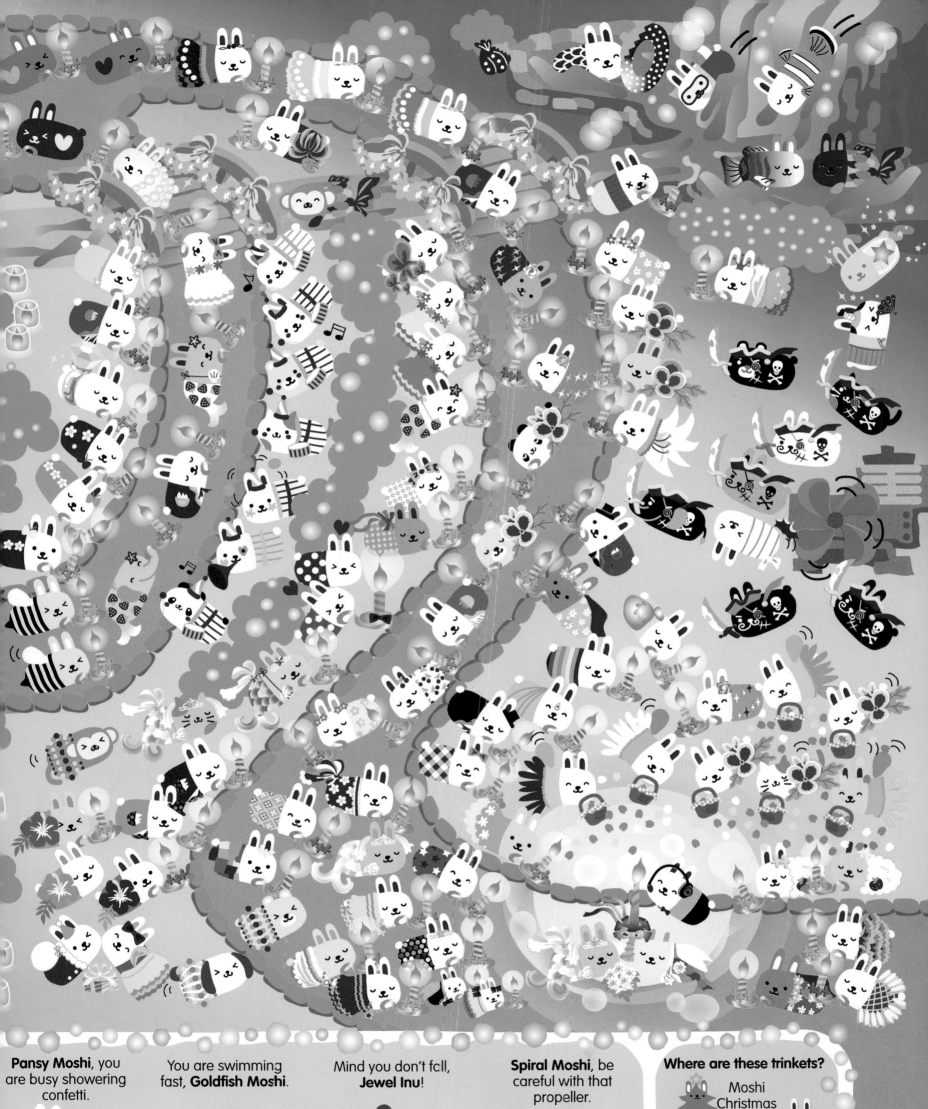

The Whirlpool

Suddenly there's complete panic as Spiral Moshi captures everyone in a whirlpool.

Where is **Strawberry Mermaid Moshi?**

Where is **Mermaid Bride Moshi?**

Where are these Moshi?

Oto-hime Moshi, you are running after something.

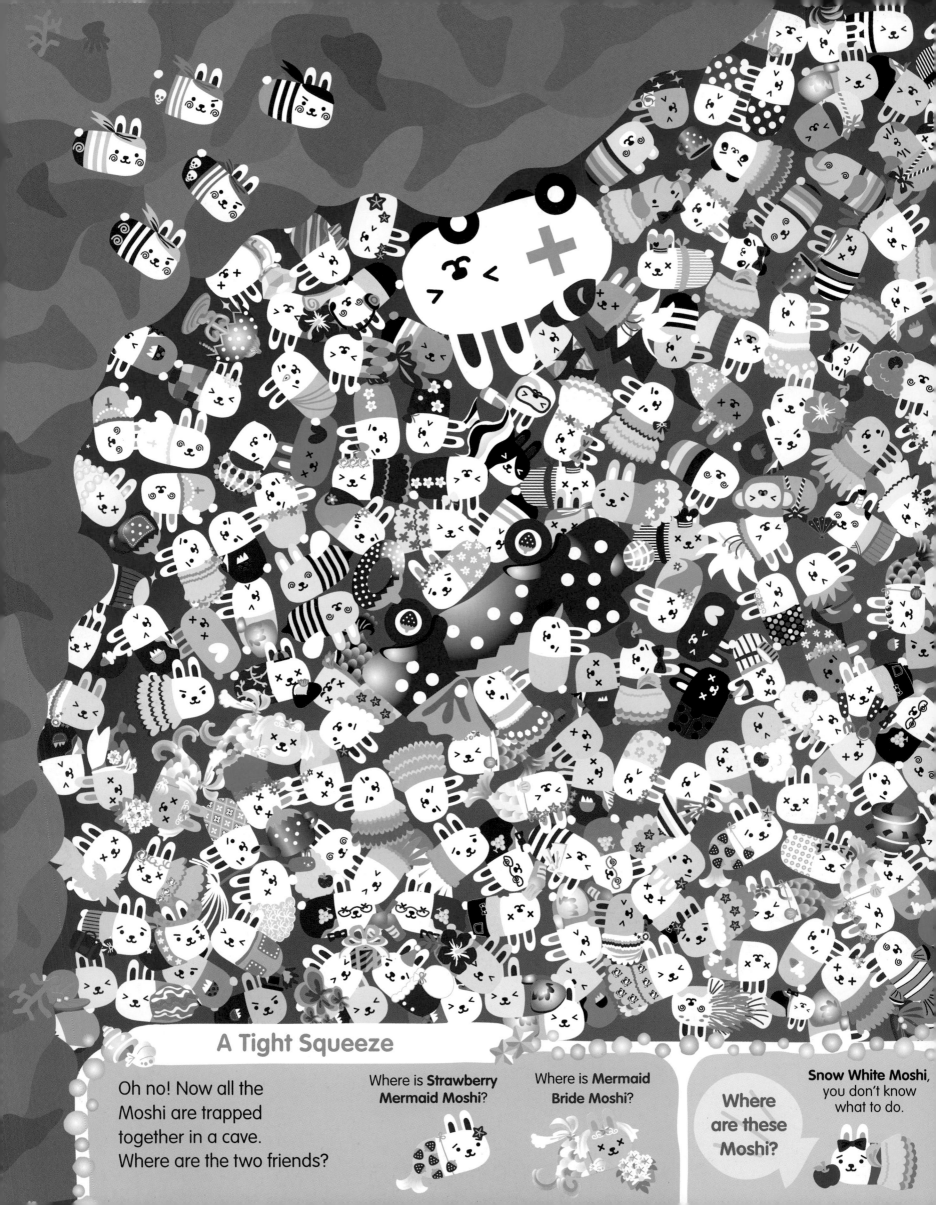

A Tight Squeeze

Oh no! Now all the Moshi are trapped together in a cave. Where are the two friends?

Where is **Strawberry Mermaid Moshi?**

Where is **Mermaid Bride Moshi?**

Where are these Moshi?

Snow White Moshi, you don't know what to do.

Frill Moshi, you are not happy.

You look dizzy, **Rainbow Moshi.**

Present Inu, you seem surprised.

Magician Moshi, you are casting a spell.

Where are these trinkets?
Moshi Skull

Moshi Shaved Ice

The Magical Take-Off

Magician Moshi has given everyone magic wings so they can fly off and escape the Spiral Moshi.

Where is **Strawberry Mermaid Moshi?**

Where is **Mermaid Bride Moshi?**

Where are these Moshi?

Enjoy the flight, **Dandelion Moshi.**

ee Moshi, help the sleeping Princess Moshi.

Have you found your sweetheart, **Super Moshi**?

Cupid Kuma, you are having fun.

Fairy Moshi, you are setting off a party popper.

Where are these trinkets?

Moshi Parachute

Moshi Ribbon Balloon

At last . . .

Mermaid Bride Moshi and Mermaid Groom Moshi set off on their honeymoon.

Moshi
Love Stories

Bikini Moshi

The Underwater Chapel

Bikini Moshi bumps into Surfboard Moshi by accident.

The Flower Petal Walk

Surfboard Moshi asks if she is all right.

Wedding Dress Emporium

Bikini Moshi thinks Surfboard Moshi is lovely.

The Busy Kitchen

She wishes he would notice her.

The Wedding Banquet

She only has eyes for him.

The Candlelit Garden

Surfboard Moshi speaks to her at last.

The Whirlpool

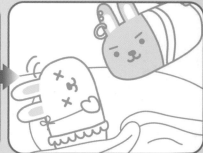

She plucks up courage to tell him she likes him.

Total Whiteout

A big wave carries them off.

A Tight Squeeze

"Hold on to me," he tells her.

The Magical Take-Off

The two are happy together.

The Moonlight Honeymoon

They stay by each other's side.

Follow the love stories of Bikini Moshi and High School Moshi, from The Underwater Chapel to The Moonlight Honeymoon.

High School Moshi

The Underwater Chapel

High School Moshi doesn't want to ride in TV Star Moshi's car.

The Flower Petal Walk

She prefers Clover Moshi, who tells funny stories.

Wedding Dress Emporium

And Camera Moshi, who takes her picture.

The Busy Kitchen

She likes Sommelier Moshi when he treats her to a glass of juice.

The Wedding Banquet

Ladybird Moshi is good fun to dance with.

The Candlelit Garden

TV Star Moshi tries talking to her again.

The Whirlpool

High School Moshi phones Student Moshi for advice.

Total Whiteout

Suddenly Robot Moshi jostles meanly into High School Moshi.

A Tight Squeeze

TV Star Moshi comes to her rescue.

The Magical Take-Off

She sees TV Star Moshi in a new light.

The Moonlight Honeymoon

The two go for a romantic drive in the night sky.

Keep on searching!

Santa Moshi

Santa Moshi is always bringing presents…

The Underwater Chapel	The Flower Petal Walk	Wedding Dress Emporium	The Busy Kitchen	The Wedding Banquet
to Cherry Blossom Moshi	to Choirboy Moshi	to Shop Assistant Moshi	to Kindergarten Moshi	to Tuxedo Moshi

Injury Moshi

Injury Moshi bumps into something wherever he goes…

The Underwater Chapel	The Flower Petal Walk	Wedding Dress Emporium	The Busy Kitchen	The Wedding Banquet
into a pillar	into a chair	into a mirror	into a pile of firewood	into a stash of presents

Silk Moshi

Silk Moshi is always eating…

The Underwater Chapel	The Flower Petal Walk	Wedding Dress Emporium	The Busy Kitchen	The Wedding Banquet
a strawberry	a cake	an ice cream	spaghetti	a steak

Polka Dot Moshi

Polka Dot Moshi is always with her boyfriend…

The Underwater Chapel	The Flower Petal Walk	Wedding Dress Emporium	The Busy Kitchen	The Wedding Banquet
toasting the wedding	dreaming together	posing with a ribbon	cooking together	sharing a glass of juice

Look for the strawberry design and find these trinkets in every scene.

 Strawberry Cup

 Strawberry Book

 Strawberry Teapot

 Strawberry Treasure Chest

 Strawberry Conch

 Strawberry Rubber Ring

 Strawberry Lamp